Outsourced Thinking

*How Systems, Feeds, and Algorithms Now Shape
What We Feel, Fear, and Believe*

Outsourced Thinking

*How Systems, Feeds, and Algorithms Now Shape
What We Feel, Fear, and Believe*

Outsourced Thinking:
How Systems, Feeds, and Algorithms Now Shape
What We Feel, Fear, and Believe

Richard Rawson, Psy.D., MBA

© 2026 Richard Rawson
All rights reserved.

No part of this book may be reproduced, stored, or transmitted in any form or by any means without the prior written permission of the author, except for brief quotations used in reviews or scholarly works.

This book is intended for educational and informational purposes only. It does not constitute professional, legal, or clinical advice.

ISBN: 979-8-9946881-6-8

Published by Rawson Internet Marketing.
United States of America.

Table of Contents

Chapter 1: When Systems Stop Being Neutral 1

Chapter 2: From Information to Regulation 9

Chapter 3: The Hidden Work of Inner Life 15

Chapter 4: Outsourced Judgement 21

Chapter 5: Algorithmic Salience 27

Chapter 6: Reaction Before Reflection 33

Chapter 7: The External Rhythm of Emotion 39

Chapter 8: The System-Driven Sense of Urgency 45

Chapter 9: Moral Attention as a Managed Resource 51

Chapter 10: When Delegated Judgment Feels Like Your Own . 57

Chapter 11: Emotional Validation by Design 63

Chapter 12: Platform-Mediated Identity Cues 69

Chapter 13: Emotional Exhaustion Without Obvious Cause . . 75

Chapter 14: Loss of Internal Pacing 81

Chapter 15: The Fragility of System-Regulated Inner Life . . 85

Chapter 16: Reclaiming Cognitive and Emotional Agency . . 91

WHEN SYSTEMS STOP BEING NEUTRAL

CHAPTER 1
When Systems Stop Being Neutral

WHEN SYSTEMS STOP BEING NEUTRAL

When Systems Stop Being Neutral

For a long time, systems were treated as background. They were tools, channels, or conveniences that helped people accomplish tasks more efficiently. A search engine helped locate information. A feed displayed what others had posted. A platform delivered messages, news, or entertainment at greater speed and scale than earlier media. The system itself was assumed to be neutral, and any problems were usually framed as misuse, bias in content, or bad actors exploiting an otherwise passive structure. That assumption rested on the idea that systems merely carried material produced elsewhere and did not meaningfully shape how it was encountered.

That assumption no longer holds because the role of systems has changed. What has shifted is not simply their reach or their technical sophistication, but their function. Systems now participate in shaping experience itself. They no longer just transmit material produced elsewhere. They organize attention, pace exposure, and condition response by deciding what appears first, what repeats, and what quietly disappears. They decide what surfaces, what recedes, and what never appears at all. In doing so, they move quietly from being tools people use to environments people inhabit.

Neutrality made sense when systems behaved like pipes. Pipes do not care what flows through them. They do not alter timing, emphasis, or emotional tone. A book does not reorder itself while it is being read. A newspaper does not study yesterday's reader reactions and reshape tomorrow's front page for each individual. Even broadcast television, for all its influence, delivers the same sequence to everyone, regardless of who is watching or how they respond.

Modern systems behave differently because they respond to the people using them. They track what draws attention, what provokes reaction, what sustains engagement, and what leads to withdrawal. They adjust continuously, modifying presentation based on observed behavior. Over time, they do not merely reflect preferences. They help produce them. What begins as responsiveness gradually becomes guidance, and what begins as personalization becomes regulation.

When Systems Stop Being Neutral

Neutrality ends when a system actively participates in deciding what matters. This is not a philosophical claim about intention or values. It is a practical description of function. When a system influences which topics recur, which emotions are reinforced, which concerns feel urgent, and which fade from awareness, it is no longer just delivering information. It is shaping what stands out, what feels important, and what draws emotional weight before deliberate judgment has time to form.

Most people experience this shift indirectly. They notice that certain topics seem to follow them across days, that emotional tones repeat without a clear connection to their own situation, and that concern often appears before deliberate thought. Many feel pulled into reactions they did not consciously choose. These experiences are often attributed to personal weakness, distraction, or lack of discipline. What is less visible is that the environment itself has changed.

In earlier contexts, attention was primarily self-directed. It was limited by time, physical access, and social boundaries. Emotional pacing was largely internal. People decided when to dwell on something, when to disengage, and when to return to it. External inputs mattered, but they arrived with friction. There were pauses, delays, and gaps that allowed experience to settle before another stimulus arrived.

Systems reduce friction by design. That reduction is part of what makes them useful. Faster access, smoother transitions, and immediate availability all remove barriers that once slowed interaction. But when friction disappears almost entirely, something else disappears with it. The space where interpretation and judgment normally occur begins to shrink.

A neutral system would deliver information and stop there. A non-neutral system continues. It monitors response, adjusts output, and optimizes for further engagement. It learns which stimuli accelerate reaction and which slow it down, and it increasingly favors the former. Over time, this creates a feedback loop in which the system becomes involved in regulating the user's internal state, even if that regulation is never named or acknowledged.

This regulation is rarely experienced as coercion. It does not usually feel imposed. Instead, it presents itself as relevance. The feed shows what seems timely.

Outsourced Thinking

The notification arrives when attention dips. The headline appears just as emotional intensity begins to wane. Each moment feels coincidental, even helpful. Taken together, however, these moments create direction.

Systems do not need intent to exert influence. They do not require beliefs, ideology, or moral commitments. Optimization alone is sufficient. When a system is designed to maximize engagement, it will surface material that reliably generates response. Response is not neutral. Certain emotional states produce stronger signals than others. Anxiety, anger, fear, and moral outrage generate more consistent engagement than calm reflection or sustained uncertainty. As a result, they appear more often.

This does not require malice. It requires measurement. Once measurement exists, neutrality erodes. The system is no longer indifferent to outcome. It is structured to favor some patterns of attention and emotion over others. Even if no human editor selects the material, selection still occurs. The mechanism replaces discretion. The logic replaces judgment.

What makes this shift difficult to recognize is that it operates below the level of explicit belief. People do not experience systems telling them what to think. They experience systems telling them what to notice. That distinction matters because beliefs can be challenged, while attention often cannot. By the time conscious evaluation begins, the terrain has already been shaped.

When a system repeatedly surfaces certain themes, issues, or emotional tones, those elements acquire weight. They feel important because they are present. They feel urgent because they recur. They feel personal because they arrive in proximity to one's own reactions. Over time, the boundary between external input and internal concern becomes harder to locate.

This is why explanations that focus only on bias often miss the point. Bias suggests distortion of truth. What is happening here is more basic. The system is not deciding what is true. It is deciding what is visible. It is not telling people what to believe. It is influencing what they attend to, and how often they encounter it.

Visibility precedes belief. What stands out precedes judgment. By the time reasoning begins, the conditions under which it occurs have already been structured.

The shift from neutrality to regulation also alters responsibility. In a neutral environment, individuals are expected to manage their own reactions. They choose when to engage, when to withdraw, and how much weight to give a stimulus. In a regulated environment, those decisions are increasingly shared with the system. Timing, intensity, and focus are subtly suggested through pattern and repetition.

As this delegation increases, internal capacities change. Skills that were once practiced regularly, such as tolerating ambiguity, pacing concern, or delaying reaction, are used less often. The system handles sorting and prioritization. The individual responds.

This is not a moral failing. It is an adaptation. Humans adjust to the environments they inhabit. When attention is continuously guided, self-guidance weakens. When emotional cues are externally paced, internal pacing becomes less practiced.

The non-neutral role of systems becomes especially visible when they change. A platform alters its algorithm, and people report shifts in mood, concern, or engagement that seem disproportionate to any specific content difference. What they are experiencing is a disruption in rhythm. The familiar pacing has moved, and the emotional scaffolding shifts with it.

If systems were truly neutral, these internal adjustments would not register so strongly at the level of felt experience. The fact that they do suggests that systems have already been doing more than delivering material. They have been shaping the conditions under which experience unfolds.

Recognizing this shift does not require rejecting technology or idealizing earlier eras. It requires acknowledging that the psychological role of systems has changed. They are no longer external to inner life. They interact with it continuously, often without being noticed.

Once systems stop being neutral, new questions follow naturally. Who sets the priorities embedded in optimization? What emotional patterns are reinforced by default? Which forms of attention become harder to sustain over time? And what happens to judgment when the ground beneath it is already in motion?

Those questions cannot be answered by examining content alone. They require attention to structure, timing, and feedback. They require seeing systems not as passive conduits, but as active organizers of experience. Everything that follows in this book begins with that recognition.

FROM INFORMATION TO REGULATION

CHAPTER 2
From Information to Regulation

From Information To Regulation

From Information to Regulation

For most of modern history, information was treated as something people received and then acted on. A newspaper delivered facts. A report summarized findings. A broadcast conveyed events. What people did with that information was assumed to be their responsibility. They interpreted it, evaluated its relevance, decided whether it mattered, and determined how to respond. Information influenced behavior, but it did not manage it.

That distinction has blurred. Systems increasingly do more than provide information. They shape the conditions under which information is encountered, interpreted, and acted upon. They do not stop at delivery. They continue into sequencing, emphasis, repetition, and timing. In doing so, they begin to regulate response rather than simply inform judgment.

Regulation does not require explicit rules. It does not need instructions, warnings, or commands. It operates through structure. When a system decides what appears first, what appears often, and what disappears quickly, it is influencing behavior before conscious choice enters the picture. The user still reacts freely, but the range and rhythm of possible reactions have already been shaped.

This shift is subtle because it feels like an extension of relevance. Systems promise to show what matters most. They filter abundance into manageable streams. They remove noise. In practice, however, relevance is never neutral. It is defined by metrics, and metrics reward some outcomes more reliably than others. When relevance is calculated rather than chosen, the system becomes an intermediary between experience and response.

Earlier information environments relied on internal regulation. People learned to skim, to ignore, to pause, and to return later. They learned to tolerate not knowing, to hold competing ideas without resolving them immediately, and to decide when a response was warranted. These skills were imperfect, but they were exercised regularly because nothing else could perform them.

Systems now perform much of this work externally. They decide when something deserves attention, how long it should remain visible, and when it should be replaced by something else. They encourage immediate reaction through prompts, alerts, and signals of activity. They reward responsiveness and penalize delay. Over time, this changes how people relate to information itself.

Information used to arrive with gaps. A story broke, and then time passed. Reactions unfolded at human pace. Conversation followed, but it did not refresh itself every few seconds. Those gaps mattered. They allowed emotions to settle and meanings to form. Without them, reaction becomes the default mode of engagement.

Regulation emerges most clearly when systems begin shaping not just what people know, but how they respond. When a headline is paired with indicators of urgency, outrage, or social approval, it does more than convey facts. It frames the appropriate emotional stance. When a topic is repeatedly resurfaced, it signals ongoing importance regardless of whether new information exists. When engagement metrics determine visibility, they quietly prioritize content that provokes reaction over content that requires reflection.

This does not mean people are being controlled in a crude sense. They still choose what to click, what to share, and what to ignore. But choice occurs within an environment that nudges certain responses forward and lets others fall away. The system does not force action. It conditions likelihood.

Over time, people begin to rely on these signals. Instead of asking whether something matters, they notice whether it is present. Instead of deciding when to respond, they respond when prompted. Instead of judging intensity, they mirror the tone already established. The system becomes a reference point for appropriate reaction.

This reliance is reinforced by volume. When information arrives continuously, the cost of independent evaluation rises. There is less time to assess context, credibility, or consequence. External cues become shortcuts. They offer guidance without effort. In high-volume environments, shortcuts are not laziness. They are survival strategies.

As systems take on regulatory roles, responsibility subtly shifts. Emotional escalation feels less like a personal choice and more like a natural response to circumstances. Urgency feels self-evident. Concern feels justified because it is shared and visible. The system distributes reassurance and alarm in alternating cycles, keeping engagement active while preventing resolution.

This pattern changes the relationship between information and meaning. Information no longer accumulates toward understanding. It circulates to maintain responsiveness. Topics return without closure. Emotions rise and fall without resolution. The system does not aim for comprehension. It aims for continuation.

Regulation also operates through absence. What is not shown carries no weight. Issues that do not generate engagement recede regardless of their significance. Slow-moving problems, complex trade-offs, and ambiguous situations struggle to remain visible. They do not disappear because they are resolved, but because they do not fit the system's regulatory logic.

This creates a mismatch between lived experience and mediated experience. People feel urgency without clear cause. They feel concern that does not align with their immediate circumstances. They feel pressure to respond even when no action is possible. The system supplies stimuli faster than meaning can form.

Over time, the line between internal motivation and external prompting becomes harder to draw. People experience reactions as their own, even when those reactions are paced and amplified by the system. The regulatory role remains invisible because it operates through familiarity rather than force.

Understanding this shift matters because regulation changes expectations. In an informational model, people are responsible for judgment. In a regulatory model, judgment is partially delegated. When outcomes feel overwhelming or exhausting, individuals blame themselves for failing to keep up, rather than recognizing that the environment has been designed to prevent equilibrium.

The move from information to regulation is easy to miss. It unfolds gradually, through convenience, optimization, and responsiveness. By the time it is noticed, it is already embedded in daily routines. People do not ask whether systems should regulate response because they no longer experience response as separable from delivery.

The chapters that follow examine what this delegation does to inner life. They trace how attention, judgment, emotion, and moral concern become increasingly shaped by systems that were never named as regulators, but now function as such.

CHAPTER 3

The Hidden Work of Inner Life

The Hidden Work of Inner Life

Psychological stability depends on work people rarely notice themselves doing. Attention has to be managed. Emotional intensity has to be contained, redirected, or allowed to pass. Meaning has to be built from incomplete and sometimes conflicting information. This work usually happens without labels or deliberate effort, which makes it easy to miss how much of it is happening at all.

Before systems took on regulatory roles, this work was unavoidable. Information arrived intermittently. Experiences unfolded at human speed. Gaps existed between stimulus and response, and those gaps were not empty. They were filled with appraisal, hesitation, comparison, and restraint. People learned, often without instruction, how to sit with uncertainty, how to decide what deserved concern, and how to let some impressions pass without action.

This labor was not evenly distributed or perfectly performed. Some people struggled more than others. Some environments made it easier, others harder. Still, the responsibility for pacing inner life rested primarily with the individual. There was no external structure continuously offering cues about what mattered most, how urgent it was, or how one ought to feel in response.

Attention required effort because it was limited. Choosing to focus on one thing meant excluding others. Distraction existed, but it did not constantly reassert itself. When attention wandered, it often did so internally, through memory or imagination, rather than being pulled outward by new inputs. This allowed for longer stretches of sustained engagement and deeper absorption.

Emotional regulation followed a similar pattern. Feelings arose in response to events, but they were tempered by time, context, and reflection. Anger cooled. Fear subsided. Excitement faded. These shifts were not signs of indifference. They were part of a natural rhythm that allowed people to remain functional without being overwhelmed by every stimulus.

Meaning-making also required work. Information did not arrive pre-framed with signals about importance or moral weight. People compared new inputs to prior experience. They discussed them with others. They revised interpretations over time. Meaning was provisional, and that provisional quality allowed for adjustment.

This internal labor depended on friction. Delays mattered. Waiting mattered. Not knowing mattered. When answers were unavailable or incomplete, people learned to tolerate ambiguity. When outcomes were uncertain, they learned to hold competing possibilities without resolving them immediately. These capacities were not taught explicitly, but they were exercised regularly because circumstances demanded them.

The effort involved was rarely acknowledged. People did not think of themselves as performing cognitive or emotional labor simply by living their lives. The work was embedded in daily routines. It was part of reading, listening, conversing, and deciding. Because it was continuous, it became normalized.

What changes when systems assume parts of this work is not just behavior, but skill. Skills that are not used regularly tend to weaken. When external structures take over pacing, sorting, and prioritization, internal capacities are exercised less often. This does not mean they disappear, but they become less reliable under strain.

Consider attention. When a system decides what appears next, how long it stays visible, and when it should be replaced, the effort of choosing focus diminishes. Attention becomes reactive rather than intentional. The person still experiences focus, but it is guided. Over time, sustaining attention without external prompts becomes harder because the internal muscles have not been trained under load.

The same applies to emotional modulation. When systems amplify certain emotional cues and dampen others, they alter the range of feelings that are practiced. Rapid shifts between alarm and reassurance become familiar. Slower processes, such as gradual acceptance or unresolved tension, receive less reinforcement. Emotional rhythms begin to match system rhythms rather than lived experience.

Meaning-making is affected as well. When systems attach signals of importance to information, they reduce the need for personal appraisal. Topics feel significant because they recur, not because they have been weighed. Moral reactions feel appropriate because they are mirrored, not because they have been examined. The work of interpretation is partially outsourced.

This outsourcing feels efficient. It reduces cognitive load in the short term. Decisions feel easier. Responses feel justified. The system appears to be helping by narrowing choices and clarifying priorities. What is less visible is the long-term cost of reduced practice.

Without regular engagement in internal pacing, tolerance for ambiguity declines. Uncertainty becomes uncomfortable more quickly. Delayed resolution feels intolerable. The absence of clear signals produces anxiety rather than curiosity. People begin to seek external cues not because they lack intelligence or discipline, but because their environment has trained them to expect guidance.

This helps explain why many people feel overwhelmed even when their objective demands have not increased. The exhaustion does not come from too much thinking, but from too little self-directed regulation. When internal systems are underused, they fatigue quickly when called upon. What once felt manageable now feels draining.

The hidden work of inner life also includes deciding what not to care about. Indifference is often framed negatively, but selective disengagement is essential for psychological health. No person can respond fully to every stimulus. Choosing where to invest concern requires boundaries. Those boundaries were once formed through experience and reflection.

Systems make disengagement harder by design. When inputs are continuous and personalized, absence feels like neglect. Ignoring a signal feels like missing something important. The pressure to remain responsive undermines the ability to step back and let issues resolve without intervention.

As this pressure accumulates, people experience a sense of constant partial engagement. They are never fully immersed, but never fully disengaged. Attention is fragmented. Emotions are activated without resolution. Meaning remains provisional without settling. This state consumes energy even when no specific task is demanding it.

Recognizing the hidden work of inner life clarifies what is at stake in the shift toward system regulation. The issue is not that systems provide information or convenience. It is that they increasingly perform functions that were once essential training grounds for psychological resilience.

When those functions are externalized, people lose opportunities to practice them. The result is not ignorance, but fragility. Inner systems become dependent on outer scaffolding. When that scaffolding shifts, overloads, or disappears, the individual feels unprepared to compensate.

The next step in this progression involves judgment itself. Once attention, emotion, and pacing are partially delegated, decisions about what deserves evaluation begin to follow. That transition marks a deeper form of outsourcing, one that reshapes not just experience, but agency itself.

CHAPTER 4

Outsourced Judgment

OUTSOURCED JUDGMENT

Outsourced Judgment

Judgment is not a single act. It is a sequence of decisions that usually unfolds without much attention. Something appears. It is noticed or ignored. If it is noticed, it is evaluated. If it is evaluated, it may trigger concern, interest, or action. Most of the time, people do not experience this as a deliberate process. It feels immediate and intuitive, even though it depends on many small choices happening in quick succession.

For much of everyday life, these choices were made internally. People decided what was worth their time, what could wait, and what did not require response at all. They weighed relevance against obligation and urgency against capacity. These judgments were imperfect, but they were practiced constantly, which made them flexible and adaptive.

As systems take on regulatory roles, they begin influencing this process at its earliest stages. Before a person evaluates something, the system decides whether it appears. Before concern arises, the system determines how often the stimulus is repeated and in what context. By the time conscious judgment begins, much of the sorting has already occurred.

This is the core of outsourced judgment. The system does not tell people what to think. It decides what enters the field of evaluation in the first place. It determines what is presented as needing attention and what remains invisible. That decision shapes response more powerfully than any explicit argument could.

When judgment is internal, absence has meaning. If something does not come to mind, it is assumed to be resolved, irrelevant, or outside one's responsibility. When judgment is mediated by systems, absence loses that meaning. What is absent may simply not have been selected. People learn, often unconsciously, to treat presence as a signal of importance.

This shift changes how concern is allocated. Instead of asking whether something deserves attention, people respond to whether it appears repeatedly. Frequency replaces deliberation. Visibility replaces evaluation. Over time, this alters the sense of responsibility. Concern feels reactive rather than chosen.

At the same time, outsourced judgment often feels helpful. Having priorities pre-sorted reduces effort. It lowers the cognitive cost of deciding what deserves response in environments where information arrives faster than it can be evaluated. When systems signal importance, they provide orientation. They offer a sense that attention is being used efficiently rather than wasted.

This can be experienced as relief. Judgment involves uncertainty, trade-offs, and the risk of getting things wrong. External cues simplify that burden. They narrow the field of concern and reduce ambiguity about what matters most. In complex environments, this can feel stabilizing rather than constraining.

There is also emotional payoff. When concern is externally validated, response feels justified. People experience alignment between their reactions and the surrounding environment. That alignment reduces self-doubt and eases the discomfort of having to decide alone. Outsourced judgment offers reassurance that one's attention and concern are appropriate.

Systems reinforce this by coupling visibility with cues for response. Metrics, notifications, prompts, and indicators of activity suggest when engagement is expected. These cues do not force action, but they narrow the range of plausible non-responses. Ignoring a signal begins to feel like neglect rather than choice.

The result is a redistribution of judgment. The individual still reacts, but the system determines the menu of reactions. People experience themselves as deciding, but the conditions of decision-making are increasingly prearranged. What feels like personal concern often originates as system-generated priority.

This outsourcing is reinforced by speed. When stimuli arrive faster than they can be evaluated, triage becomes necessary. External cues offer a solution. They reduce the effort required to decide what matters. In high-volume environments, relying on those cues is not irrational. It is adaptive.

Over time, however, reliance becomes dependency. The capacity to evaluate independently weakens when it is used less often. People grow less confident in their own sense of priority. They check signals to confirm whether concern is warranted. Judgment shifts from being an internal process to being something verified externally.

This affects moral response as well. Systems influence not only what feels urgent, but what feels condemnable, admirable, or deserving of response. When moral signals are attached to visibility, ethical judgment becomes reactive. People feel pressure to align with the tone already established.

What is lost in this process is not intelligence or values, but discretion. Discretion requires space. It requires the ability to pause, to weigh competing demands, and to decide that some things do not require response. Systems reduce that space by presenting continuous prompts for evaluation.

Outsourced judgment also alters emotional burden. When systems decide what deserves concern, individuals are exposed to problems far beyond their capacity to influence. The resulting sense of obligation without agency creates strain. People feel responsible without knowing how to respond effectively.

This strain is often misinterpreted as apathy or burnout. In reality, it reflects a mismatch between the scope of concern and the scope of action. Judgment has been expanded without a corresponding increase in capacity.

Recognizing outsourced judgment does not require rejecting systems. It requires understanding where judgment now occurs. When systems decide what enters awareness, they shape concern before conscious evaluation begins. Agency remains, but it operates within boundaries that are rarely examined.

The next step in this progression involves salience itself: the process by which certain things come to feel important, visible, and worthy of emotional investment. Once systems influence what is evaluated, they begin shaping not just attention, but the sense of what matters at all. That shift marks a deeper reorganization of attention, one that operates continuously and often without notice.

CHAPTER 5
Algorithmic Salience

Algorithmic Salience

Salience is not about what is true. It is about what stands out. It describes the process by which certain things come to feel noticeable, important, and emotionally charged, while others recede into the background. People rarely choose salience directly. They experience it. Something feels pressing. Something else feels negligible. Attention follows that feeling long before reasoning begins.

In earlier environments, salience emerged slowly. It was shaped by proximity, repetition over time, personal relevance, and shared social focus. What mattered tended to be what persisted, what affected daily life, or what was reinforced through sustained conversation. Salience was imperfect, but it was grounded in lived rhythms.

Feeds alter this process. Algorithmic systems do not wait for importance to emerge. They produce it. By controlling what appears, how often it appears, and in what emotional context, they shape what feels worthy of attention in real time. Salience becomes a function of system behavior rather than lived experience.

This does not require deception or manipulation. It follows directly from optimization. Systems are designed to surface content that generates response. Response is measurable. Attention, engagement, and emotional reaction provide signals that can be tracked, compared, and amplified. Content that reliably produces these signals is favored. Content that does not fades, regardless of its significance.

As a result, importance becomes decoupled from consequence. Something can feel urgent without affecting daily life. Something else can be consequential but remain invisible because it does not generate reaction. Over time, this skews the internal map people use to decide what they care about.

Algorithmic salience works through repetition. What appears once may register briefly. What appears repeatedly begins to feel important. Repetition substitutes for evaluation. Familiarity substitutes for relevance. When the same themes, conflicts, or emotional tones return again and again, they acquire weight simply by being present.

It also works through clustering. Related items appear together, reinforcing a sense of coherence and momentum. Attention is drawn not to isolated facts, but to patterns constructed by the system. These patterns feel meaningful even when they are assembled for engagement rather than understanding.

Emotional framing amplifies this effect. Content is rarely neutral in tone. It arrives paired with signals that suggest how it should be felt. Urgency, outrage, reassurance, and validation are embedded in presentation. These cues guide emotional investment before conscious appraisal begins.

Over time, people internalize these signals. They learn what kinds of topics arrive with intensity and which arrive quietly, if at all. They learn what emotions are reinforced and which dissipate without acknowledgment. Emotional investment begins to track system emphasis rather than personal judgment.

This reshapes attention in subtle ways. People feel drawn toward what is highlighted and restless when it disappears. They experience concern as something that arises naturally, even when it has been externally paced. What feels important feels self-evident because it has already been filtered and emphasized.

Algorithmic salience also compresses time. Issues surface abruptly, peak quickly, and are replaced before resolution occurs. Emotional investment is intense but brief. Attention moves on not because understanding has been reached, but because the system has shifted focus. This creates a sense of constant motion without progress.

The result is a chronic state of partial engagement. People care deeply, but briefly. They feel informed, but unsettled. They respond, but rarely arrive at closure. Salience cycles faster than meaning can form.

This pattern affects not only what people notice, but how they experience responsibility. When importance is externally assigned, obligation feels externally imposed. People feel pulled toward issues they did not choose and powerless to resolve. Emotional investment accumulates without corresponding agency.

At the same time, algorithmic salience offers reassurance. When many people appear to care about the same things at the same time, concern feels validated. Emotional responses feel shared rather than idiosyncratic. This alignment reduces doubt and reinforces participation.

The cost of that reassurance is autonomy. When salience is externally managed, internal priority-setting weakens. People rely on visibility to tell them what matters. Absence becomes ambiguous rather than calming. What is not highlighted feels unresolved rather than complete.

This does not mean people lose the capacity for independent judgment. It means that judgment operates on terrain that has already been shaped. Attention arrives pre-weighted. Emotional energy is directed before reflection begins. Agency remains, but it is exercised within boundaries that are rarely examined.

Algorithmic salience is powerful precisely because it is not experienced as control. It feels like relevance. It feels like awareness. It feels like being informed. The system does not argue. It repeats. It does not persuade. It emphasizes.

Once importance itself is shaped this way, the pace of reaction changes. Reflection feels slow. Delay feels irresponsible. Emotional immediacy becomes the default mode of engagement. This sets the stage for the next shift: a growing tendency to react before thinking, even when people value careful judgment.

That tendency is not a failure of will. It is a predictable result of an environment that continually organizes what comes first.

REACTION BEFORE REFLECTION

CHAPTER 6

Reaction Before Reflection

REACTION BEFORE REFLECTION

Reaction Before Reflection

Most people believe they prefer to think before reacting. They value deliberation and want their responses to feel measured, proportionate, and grounded in understanding. When they react quickly or emotionally, they often describe it as a lapse, a momentary failure of discipline, or evidence that something bypassed their better judgment.

What feels like failure is more accurately a mismatch between preference and environment. People are not suddenly less reflective. They are operating within conditions that favor speed over pause and immediacy over evaluation. The sequence of response has been altered, not the underlying values.

In earlier contexts, delay was built into communication. Messages arrived with gaps. Information moved slowly enough that appraisal could occur alongside reception. Emotional response unfolded in parallel with interpretation rather than ahead of it. Even when reactions were strong, there was time for them to be shaped by reflection before they solidified into judgment.

Algorithmic environments reverse that sequence. Systems are designed to register and respond to reaction, not reflection. Reaction is measurable. It produces signals that can be tracked, compared, and optimized. Reflection produces little data. A pause registers as inactivity. A delayed response offers no immediate feedback. As a result, systems favor stimuli that elicit fast emotional engagement and deliver them in ways that minimize hesitation.

This does not mean people stop thinking. It means thinking is displaced in time. Emotional response arrives first, cued by framing, tone, repetition, and social signals. By the time conscious reflection begins, the emotional stance has already been set. Reflection then works to justify, adjust, or contain a response that is already underway.

Immediate emotion also feels authentic in a way that slower judgment often does not. Because it arises quickly and without apparent calculation, it is experienced as honest and unfiltered. People trust these reactions precisely because they feel spontaneous. The absence of deliberation is taken as evidence of sincerity rather than as a sign that context or consequence has not yet been considered.

This sense of authenticity strengthens the pull toward reaction. Acting quickly feels like expressing what one truly feels, while pausing can feel artificial or performative. Reflection risks being interpreted, by oneself or others, as rationalization rather than understanding. In environments that reward immediacy, emotional speed becomes associated with integrity.

People experience this as being pulled rather than choosing. The pull is not constant, but it intensifies under certain conditions. High volume increases it by reducing available attention. Emotional framing accelerates it by narrowing interpretive range. Social visibility amplifies it by making reaction observable and delay conspicuous.

Under these conditions, reflection begins to feel risky. Pausing creates discomfort. There is a sense of falling behind or failing to register what others clearly see as important. Thoughtfulness becomes difficult to distinguish from disengagement. Reaction feels safer because it signals awareness, presence, and alignment.

Systems reinforce this pattern by lowering the cost of reaction and raising the cost of delay. Responding is easy and produces immediate feedback. Reflection requires time, sustained attention, and tolerance for uncertainty. It may lead to no visible response at all, which feels increasingly illegible in environments that reward continuous engagement.

Over time, this alters internal timing. People become accustomed to responding before they fully understand what they are responding to. Emotional activation becomes the entry point rather than the outcome of judgment. Reflection still occurs, but it is compressed, deferred, or layered on top of an already active response.

This shift helps explain why people often feel regret after reacting, even when the reaction felt appropriate in the moment. The discomfort does not come from having emotions. It comes from realizing that reflection arrived too late to guide them. What follows is self-criticism rather than recognition of the conditions that shaped the sequence.

Reaction before reflection is not a personal flaw. It is a predictable response to systems that privilege immediacy and visibility. When environments reward speed, emotional immediacy becomes the default mode of engagement. Slower thinking is still valued, but it is increasingly difficult to access at the moment it would matter most.

The chapters that follow examine how this altered timing affects emotional rhythm more broadly. Once reaction consistently precedes reflection, cycles of feeling begin to align with system pacing rather than internal regulation. What feels like volatility is often synchronization with an external tempo that never fully settles.

THE EXTERNAL RHYTHM OF EMOTION

CHAPTER 7
The External Rhythm of Emotion

THE EXTERNAL RHYTHM OF EMOTION

The External Rhythm of Emotion

Emotional life has always had a rhythm. Feelings rise and fall. Intensity builds, peaks, and subsides. In earlier environments, that rhythm was shaped primarily by lived events, social interaction, and internal regulation. Emotions followed experience, and while they could be disrupted, their pacing was largely anchored to the tempo of daily life.

That anchor has weakened. When systems regulate attention and prioritize reaction, they also begin to pace emotion. Emotional intensity no longer tracks events alone. It tracks exposure. What people feel, how strongly they feel it, and how long it lasts increasingly depend on how stimuli are presented, repeated, and replaced. Emotion becomes synchronized with system timing rather than internal settling.

This synchronization does not feel imposed. It feels natural because it happens gradually. Emotional cues arrive embedded in content, framed by urgency or reassurance, and reinforced through repetition. The system establishes a tempo by determining when emotions should accelerate and when they should release. Over time, people adjust to that tempo without noticing the adjustment.

Earlier emotional rhythms included recovery. After periods of concern or excitement, there were intervals of calm. Attention shifted to routine matters. Emotional energy dissipated through action, conversation, or rest. Those intervals were not empty. They allowed feelings to integrate into understanding and return to baseline.

System-paced environments compress or eliminate those intervals. Emotional peaks arrive in rapid succession. Before one response has time to resolve, another stimulus appears. Relief follows alarm, but only briefly. Reassurance is quickly replaced by a new cause for concern. The cycle continues without settling.

This creates a pattern of oscillation. Anger rises, then gives way to validation. Fear spikes, then recedes into temporary relief. Outrage is followed by affirmation, then replaced by the next provocation. Each shift feels justified in isolation.

Together, they form a continuous loop.

Because this loop is externally paced, emotional regulation becomes reactive. People adjust to what appears next rather than to what they have already felt. Emotional processing is interrupted. Feelings are activated and deactivated before they can be fully understood. What remains is intensity without integration.

The rhythm is reinforced by visibility. When many people appear to be reacting at once, emotion feels collective. Shared reaction amplifies intensity and shortens recovery. Calm becomes socially invisible. Emotional neutrality carries no signal. The system highlights movement, not rest.

Over time, this affects baseline mood. Even in the absence of immediate stressors, people feel keyed up, unsettled, or alert. Emotional readiness replaces emotional stability. The nervous system adapts to expect frequent shifts rather than gradual change.

This state is exhausting, but the exhaustion is often misattributed. People assume they are overworked, under-resilient, or emotionally fragile. What they are experiencing is sustained exposure to externally paced emotional cycles that do not allow for completion.

The external rhythm of emotion also alters how people interpret their own feelings. Because emotions rise and fall quickly, they are experienced as transient but intense. Concern feels urgent in the moment, then oddly distant soon after. This instability undermines confidence in one's own emotional signals.

As a result, people look outward for confirmation. They check whether others are still reacting, whether the issue remains visible, whether emotional cues persist. Internal signals lose authority. External rhythm becomes the reference point for how one is supposed to feel.

This reliance further entrenches the cycle. Emotional pacing is outsourced. Recovery depends on system signals rather than internal resolution. Calm arrives not when understanding has been reached, but when attention is redirected.

None of this requires people to be emotionally naive or lacking in insight. It reflects adaptation. Humans synchronize to the rhythms of their environments. When the environment accelerates emotional turnover, inner life follows.

The cost of this synchronization is depth. Feelings are experienced intensely but briefly. They are activated often but resolved rarely. Emotional life becomes wide but shallow, busy but unfinished.

The next shift follows naturally. When emotional rhythm is externally paced and urgency is repeatedly induced, everything begins to feel pressing. Time itself feels compressed. That sense of constant urgency is not accidental. It is produced.

CHAPTER 8
The System-Driven Sense of Urgency

The System-Driven Sense of Urgency

Urgency is a feeling, not a fact. It is the sense that something requires immediate attention, that delay carries risk, and that inaction has consequences. In everyday life, urgency once arose from concrete circumstances. A deadline approached. A decision could no longer be postponed. An event unfolded faster than it could be ignored. Urgency was episodic, tied to specific situations, and resolved when action was taken or the situation passed.

That pattern has changed. In system-mediated environments, urgency is no longer anchored solely to events. It is generated continuously through exposure, pacing, and repetition. The feeling of "now" is produced even when no immediate action is possible or required. As a result, urgency becomes ambient rather than situational. It lingers without resolution.

Systems generate urgency by controlling timing. When information arrives in rapid succession, each item inherits the immediacy of the one before it. There is little distinction between what can wait and what cannot. Everything appears in the same temporal frame, competing for attention in the present moment. The result is a flattened sense of time in which all demands feel equally pressing.

This effect is amplified by cues that signal importance. Headlines framed around immediacy, notifications that interrupt ongoing activity, and indicators that others are already responding all suggest that attention is overdue. Even when no explicit instruction is given, the structure communicates haste. Delay begins to feel like failure to register reality.

Earlier environments allowed urgency to dissipate through action or understanding. A response addressed the problem. Reflection clarified priorities. Time itself reduced intensity. In system-paced environments, urgency rarely resolves. Attention shifts before resolution occurs. One urgent matter replaces another, leaving the underlying tension intact.

This creates a state of perpetual readiness. People remain alert, scanning for what demands response next. Rest does not feel restorative because it is interrupted by the expectation of return. Calm feels provisional, as though it could be revoked at any moment by the next signal.

The system-driven sense of urgency also alters judgment. When everything feels pressing, prioritization becomes difficult. Decisions are made under the impression that delay carries cost, even when that cost is undefined. Speed substitutes for clarity. Acting quickly feels responsible, while waiting feels negligent.

This pressure is reinforced socially. When others appear to be responding immediately, urgency becomes normative. Hesitation risks appearing disengaged or out of touch. The perception that "everyone else is already reacting" compresses decision time further, regardless of whether that perception reflects reality.

Over time, people internalize this tempo. Urgency becomes a baseline state rather than a response to specific conditions. Even in quiet moments, there is a sense that something is pending. Attention remains partially allocated to monitoring, rather than fully engaged with what is present.

This baseline urgency is mentally and emotionally taxing. It keeps the nervous system activated without providing a clear target for resolution. Energy is expended in anticipation rather than action. Fatigue accumulates without the satisfaction of completion.

Because the urgency feels internal, people often blame themselves. They assume they are anxious, disorganized, or failing to manage time effectively. What they are experiencing is not simply personal stress, but prolonged exposure to externally generated immediacy that never allows for closure.

The system-driven sense of urgency also narrows moral and emotional range. When everything feels immediate, there is little space for patience, nuance, or uncertainty. Complex issues are experienced as demands for instant stance rather than careful consideration. Urgency crowds out deliberation not because people reject it, but because the environment does not allow time for it to occur.

This does not mean urgency is always false or unnecessary. Some situations genuinely require immediate response. The problem arises when urgency becomes detached from consequence. When it is generated by structure rather than circumstance, it loses its signaling value. Everything feels urgent, and nothing is resolved.

As urgency becomes ambient, relief becomes rare. There is no clear point at which attention can stand down. The sense of "enough" disappears. What remains is constant partial engagement, driven not by choice, but by timing imposed from outside.

The next chapter examines how this persistent urgency reshapes moral attention itself. When systems decide what feels pressing, they also influence what people feel responsible for, condemn, or feel compelled to address. Urgency does not only pace action. It reorganizes what people care about.

CHAPTER 9

Moral Attention as a Managed Resource

Moral Attention as a Managed Resource

Moral attention refers to where people direct concern, judgment, and responsibility. It is the part of inner life that answers questions like what deserves care, what demands condemnation, and what can be set aside without guilt. In earlier contexts, moral attention was shaped by proximity, relationship, shared norms, and sustained reflection. People cared most about what touched their lives directly or what their communities held in view over time.

That pattern has shifted. When systems regulate attention and urgency, they also influence moral focus. What appears repeatedly, what arrives framed with emotional weight, and what is surrounded by visible reaction begins to feel morally significant. Concern is drawn toward what is surfaced, not necessarily toward what is most consequential or actionable. Moral attention becomes responsive to system pacing rather than to lived responsibility.

This does not mean people lose their values. It means that values are activated selectively. Systems determine which issues are presented as deserving of judgment and which pass without notice. Over time, this creates a managed moral field in which concern is concentrated, redistributed, and withdrawn according to visibility and engagement rather than deliberation.

Moral attention has limits. No one can care fully about everything. In earlier environments, those limits were acknowledged implicitly. Distance reduced obligation. Time allowed priorities to settle. Some issues were recognized as beyond individual capacity, and concern was moderated accordingly.

System-mediated environments blur those boundaries. When distant issues are delivered with immediacy and emotional framing, they feel closer than they are. When moral cues arrive continuously, restraint begins to feel like indifference. People experience pressure to register concern even when no meaningful response is possible.

Platforms reinforce this pressure by attaching moral signals to engagement. Visibility is paired with cues of approval or disapproval. Reaction becomes a proxy for care. Condemnation, affirmation, and alignment are made legible through response, while silence becomes ambiguous. Moral participation is measured, displayed, and rewarded.

This creates a feedback loop. Issues that generate strong moral reaction receive more visibility. Issues that do not provoke immediate response recede. Over time, moral attention is trained toward what produces engagement rather than what sustains understanding or leads to resolution.

The result is a narrowing of moral bandwidth. People are exposed to a succession of causes, outrages, and responsibilities without time to integrate them. Concern spikes and fades. Guilt accumulates without release. Moral energy is spent reacting rather than acting.

This pattern also affects judgment. When moral attention is externally paced, evaluation becomes compressed. Issues are framed in ways that invite immediate stance rather than careful consideration. Nuance feels out of place. Ambivalence feels suspect. Moral clarity is prized even when circumstances are complex.

Because this process feels collective, it carries authority. When many people appear to be reacting in the same way at the same time, moral judgment feels confirmed. Individuals trust their reactions more readily because they are shared. This reduces uncertainty but also discourages independent appraisal.

At the same time, moral fatigue sets in. Caring repeatedly about issues beyond one's capacity to influence creates strain. People feel responsible without being effective. Over time, this leads either to withdrawal or to hardened reactivity. Neither response reflects a lack of concern. Both reflect overload.

Systems do not manage moral attention by issuing commands. They manage it by structuring exposure. They decide which issues appear as urgent, which arrive with emotional framing, and which are reinforced through repetition. Moral significance is suggested through presence and intensity rather than through argument.

As this pattern persists, people lose confidence in their own sense of moral proportion. They look outward to determine what deserves care and how strongly it should be felt. Moral judgment becomes something to be verified rather than exercised.

This does not eliminate conscience. It relocates its cues. Internal signals are overridden by external emphasis. What feels right aligns increasingly with what is visible and reinforced. What feels permissible to ignore becomes unclear.

Understanding moral attention as a managed resource clarifies why so many people feel both morally engaged and morally exhausted. The issue is not apathy. It is overexposure without integration. Care is elicited faster than it can be resolved.

The next shift deepens this pattern. When moral attention is repeatedly activated and validated through systems, people begin to internalize system-generated priorities as their own convictions. Delegated judgment starts to feel personal, even when its origins remain external.

WHEN DELEGATED JUDGMENT FEELS LIKE YOUR OWN

CHAPTER 10

When Delegated Judgment Feels Like Your Own

When Delegated Judgment Feels Like Your Own

Delegated judgment does not usually feel delegated. It feels personal. People experience their reactions, priorities, and convictions as arising from within, even when the conditions that shaped them were external. This is not because people are confused about their inner lives, but because judgment rarely announces its origins. It presents itself as intuition, clarity, or conviction.

Earlier chapters described how systems influence what appears, what feels urgent, and what draws moral attention. The next shift occurs when those externally shaped priorities are no longer experienced as prompts, but as settled belief. At that point, delegation disappears from awareness. What began as guidance becomes identity.

This internalization happens gradually. Repeated exposure creates familiarity. Familiarity produces comfort. Over time, the emotional tone, concerns, and evaluative stance associated with a topic begin to feel natural rather than suggested. People stop noticing that their attention was directed. They only notice that they care.

Because the process is incremental, it avoids resistance. Sudden persuasion invites scrutiny. Gradual alignment does not. When priorities emerge slowly through repetition and reinforcement, they feel discovered rather than adopted. People experience themselves as arriving at conclusions independently, even when the path was structured.

System-generated priorities also gain credibility through consistency. When the same themes, concerns, or moral framings appear across contexts, they acquire the weight of coherence. Coherence is often mistaken for truth. The alignment of cues feels like confirmation rather than reinforcement.

Emotional reinforcement plays a central role. When certain reactions are repeatedly validated through visibility, affirmation, or social response, those reactions become self-trusting. People learn to recognize them as appropriate expressions of who they are. Over time, reacting in those ways feels less like participation and more like self-expression.

This is why delegated judgment can feel authentic. The emotions involved are real. The concern is sincere. The conviction is felt, not performed. What is obscured is the role of the system in shaping which feelings were practiced and which were allowed to fade.

Once internalized, system-shaped priorities are defended as personal belief. Challenges are experienced not as disagreements about emphasis, but as threats to integrity. People respond emotionally because what is being questioned feels like part of the self rather than a position adopted under certain conditions.

This fusion of judgment and identity narrows flexibility. Revising a belief begins to feel like betraying oneself. Pausing to reconsider feels like weakness. Conviction becomes a stabilizing force in environments that otherwise feel unstable, which makes it harder to relinquish even when doubt arises.

Delegated judgment also simplifies decision-making. When priorities feel settled, fewer choices need to be made. Attention flows automatically. Responses feel justified without extended deliberation. This efficiency is comforting in complex environments where constant evaluation would be exhausting.

The cost of this comfort is opacity. People lose visibility into how their priorities formed. They know what they believe, but not how those beliefs were shaped. This makes reflection harder, not because people lack insight, but because the process that produced conviction is no longer accessible to awareness.

Social reinforcement strengthens this effect. When others respond to the same cues in similar ways, internalized priorities feel confirmed. Shared conviction replaces individual evaluation. Belief feels collective and therefore secure.

At this stage, disagreement becomes more destabilizing. When judgments feel personal, critique feels intrusive. When priorities feel self-generated, questioning them feels like questioning autonomy itself. The boundary between influence and selfhood becomes difficult to locate.

This does not mean people become unthinking or dogmatic by default. It means that the environment has altered the way conviction forms. Beliefs emerge through exposure, reinforcement, and emotional alignment rather than through deliberate appraisal alone. Once formed, they are experienced as chosen even when their formation was guided.

Recognizing this process does not require abandoning conviction or distrusting every belief. It requires restoring visibility into how judgment develops. When people can see where guidance entered, they regain the ability to distinguish between what they genuinely endorse and what they have grown accustomed to endorsing.

The next chapter examines how systems actively reward some emotional expressions while discouraging others. Once judgment feels personal, emotional validation becomes a powerful force in shaping which parts of the self are reinforced and which remain underdeveloped.

CHAPTER 11

Emotional Validation By Design

Emotional Validation By Design

Emotional expression does not occur in a vacuum. People learn, over time, which emotions are welcome, which are ignored, and which carry social or psychological cost. In face-to-face settings, this learning happens through subtle cues. Tone, body language, and response shape what feels appropriate to express and what feels better contained. The feedback is imperfect, but it is usually grounded in relationship and context.

Systems change how this feedback works. When emotional expression is mediated through platforms, validation becomes structured rather than situational. Responses are quantified. Visibility is conditional. Some emotions are amplified, echoed, and rewarded, while others pass without acknowledgment or disappear entirely. Over time, this creates a patterned emotional environment that teaches people what kinds of feelings are worth expressing.

Validation no longer depends primarily on understanding or mutual recognition. It depends on engagement. Emotional expressions that generate reaction are surfaced more often. Those that do not are quietly deprioritized. The system does not evaluate emotional accuracy or appropriateness. It evaluates responsiveness.

This has consequences for how people learn to feel in public and, eventually, in private. Emotions that reliably produce acknowledgment become familiar and accessible. They are practiced more often. Emotions that receive little feedback become harder to sustain. They feel uncertain, unsupported, or incomplete.

Intensity is especially well rewarded. Strong emotions are easier to register and more likely to provoke reaction. They cut through volume and compete effectively for attention. Subtle or ambivalent emotions struggle to register in environments that privilege speed and clarity. Over time, this skews emotional expression toward what is easily legible rather than what is carefully felt.

Moralized emotions receive particularly strong reinforcement. Outrage, condemnation, and affirmation align well with system signals. They communicate stance quickly and invite response. Their clarity makes them efficient carriers of alignment. As a result, they are practiced frequently and validated consistently.

Emotions that require time or context fare less well. Confusion, doubt, mixed feeling, and quiet concern are harder to signal and slower to resolve. They do not reliably generate engagement. When they appear, they are often bypassed or flattened into simpler expressions that fit the system's feedback logic.

This does not mean people stop experiencing complex emotions. It means they stop expressing them in environments where they are not reinforced. Over time, expression shapes experience. Feelings that are not articulated or acknowledged lose coherence. They remain present, but they are less available for reflection or integration.

Because validation is externalized, people begin to associate emotional legitimacy with visibility. An emotion feels more real when it is recognized. It feels more justified when it is echoed. Silence creates uncertainty about whether a feeling is appropriate, exaggerated, or misplaced.

This dynamic encourages emotional conformity without requiring explicit pressure. People learn, often unconsciously, which emotional responses fit the environment. They adjust expression to match what is reinforced. Over time, those adjustments feel natural rather than strategic.

Emotional validation by design also affects regulation. When certain emotions are consistently rewarded, they become easier to access and harder to modulate. People reach them quickly because they are familiar and socially legible. Other emotional responses, which might be more proportionate or useful, are slower to surface because they have not been practiced under reinforcement.

This contributes to a narrowing of emotional range. Expression becomes more predictable. Emotional life feels intense but repetitive. People experience themselves as expressive, yet constrained within a limited repertoire of responses that reliably produce acknowledgment.

The absence of validation carries its own effects. When emotional expressions are ignored, people often interpret that silence as a signal about the emotion itself rather than about the system. They conclude that the feeling is unimportant, unwelcome, or illegible. This discourages further exploration and expression.

Over time, this can create a split between inner experience and outward expression. People feel things they do not know how to articulate in public spaces. Those feelings remain private, unresolved, or displaced into more acceptable forms. Emotional life becomes unevenly developed.

None of this requires systems to intend emotional shaping. The pattern emerges from structure. When engagement determines visibility, and visibility determines validation, emotional expression adapts accordingly. The system teaches without instruction.

Understanding emotional validation as designed feedback clarifies why people often feel emotionally expressive yet emotionally constrained at the same time. They are responding to an environment that rewards certain feelings consistently and others not at all. What feels like personal preference is often learned alignment.

The next chapter examines how this alignment extends beyond emotion into identity itself. When certain reactions and expressions are repeatedly validated, they begin to signal not just what one feels, but who one is supposed to be.

CHAPTER 12
Platform-Mediated Identity Cues

Platform-Mediated Identity Cues

Identity is not formed only through introspection. It develops through feedback. People learn who they are by noticing which parts of themselves are recognized, affirmed, or ignored. Over time, those signals shape what feels natural to express and what feels out of place. Identity emerges not just from inner conviction, but from repeated interaction with an environment that responds selectively.

Platforms introduce a new layer to this process. When expression is mediated through systems, feedback becomes patterned and persistent. Certain reactions are consistently rewarded with visibility and response. Certain stances appear to travel farther, linger longer, and attract affirmation. Others receive little acknowledgment or disappear quickly. These patterns act as cues, signaling which expressions fit and which do not.

Unlike explicit social norms, these cues are rarely stated. There are no rules announcing what kind of person one should be. Instead, identity guidance arrives through repetition. When a particular tone, emotion, or position reliably receives recognition, it begins to feel appropriate. When another consistently falls flat, it begins to feel misaligned. People adjust not because they are instructed to, but because the environment teaches through response.

This learning happens gradually. A person expresses a reaction and notices how it is received. Over time, patterns emerge. Certain expressions feel easier to sustain. They invite connection and reduce uncertainty about how one will be perceived. Other expressions feel awkward, unsupported, or invisible. Those require more effort and carry more risk.

As a result, people begin to associate aspects of themselves with particular reactions. Identity becomes linked to stance. Emotional expression becomes a marker of belonging. To feel aligned with oneself is increasingly to feel aligned with the cues the platform reinforces.

This does not require people to consciously shape a persona. In fact, it works best when it remains unnoticed. The adjustments feel organic. People say what feels right, and what feels right has been quietly shaped by prior reinforcement. Over time, expression and identity begin to mirror the system's preferences.

Platform-mediated identity cues also simplify complexity. Holding mixed or evolving positions is harder when identity is signaled through recognizable patterns. Consistency is rewarded. Clear stances are easier to interpret and amplify. Ambivalence, hesitation, or contradiction complicate signaling and often receive less response.

This pushes identity toward coherence over accuracy. Being legible becomes more important than being tentative. People feel pressure to maintain alignment with their prior expressions, not because they are rigid, but because inconsistency risks destabilizing how they are recognized.

Once identity cues are established, they begin to guide future behavior. People anticipate which reactions fit who they are perceived to be. They preemptively adjust expression to maintain continuity. This anticipation reduces uncertainty but narrows range. Identity becomes something to be performed consistently rather than explored.

Emotional expression is especially affected. When certain emotions align with identity cues, they become easier to access and harder to question. Other emotions feel incompatible. A person may experience them internally but hesitate to express them, even to themselves, because they do not fit the established pattern.

This creates a feedback loop. Expression reinforces identity. Identity guides expression. Over time, the distinction between preference and performance blurs. People experience themselves as choosing reactions that feel authentic, even when those reactions have been shaped by repeated environmental cues.

Platform-mediated identity cues also affect disagreement. When stances are tied to identity, shifting position feels destabilizing. Revising a view risks disrupting how one is recognized. Reflection becomes costly because it threatens continuity. The system does not enforce rigidity, but it rewards stability.

None of this means identity becomes false or manufactured. The feelings involved are real. The convictions are sincerely held. What changes is the process by which certain aspects of the self are reinforced while others remain underdeveloped. Identity becomes narrower not through coercion, but through selective recognition.

Understanding identity cues as platform-mediated helps explain why people often feel both strongly self-expressive and strangely constrained. They are expressing real parts of themselves within an environment that quietly limits which parts receive acknowledgment. Freedom of expression remains, but freedom of development is uneven.

The next chapter examines the emotional cost of this narrowing. When attention, reaction, and identity are continuously shaped by external cues, people often feel depleted without a clear reason. The exhaustion does not come from effort alone, but from sustained misalignment between inner life and externally paced expression.

CHAPTER 13

Emotional Exhaustion Without Obvious Cause

Emotional Exhaustion Without Obvious Cause

Many people describe feeling depleted without being able to point to a clear reason. They are not necessarily working longer hours. They may not be in acute crisis. Nothing dramatic has happened that would normally explain the level of fatigue they feel. And yet, motivation is low, patience is thin, and emotional reserves seem harder to access.

This exhaustion is confusing because it does not match familiar models of burnout. Traditional burnout follows effort. It is tied to sustained overwork, high stakes, or prolonged stress without relief. What people are experiencing here feels different. The tiredness is diffuse. It does not lift with rest. It persists even during periods that are supposed to be restorative.

One reason for this is that emotional energy is being spent continuously without clear endpoints. Earlier chapters described how systems pace attention, reaction, urgency, and identity. Each of these processes draws on emotional resources. When they operate occasionally, the cost is manageable. When they operate constantly, depletion accumulates.

Much of this expenditure is invisible. People are not aware that they are doing emotional work because it does not look like effort. It looks like staying informed, staying responsive, staying aligned, and staying present. None of these feel optional. Each feels minor in isolation. Together, they create sustained demand.

A major contributor to this exhaustion is unresolved activation. Emotional responses are triggered repeatedly but rarely brought to completion. Concern arises without action. Urgency spikes without resolution. Moral attention is engaged without agency. Emotions are activated and then displaced by the next stimulus before they can settle.

This pattern prevents recovery. Emotional systems are designed to cycle. Activation is followed by processing and return to baseline. When cycles are interrupted, the system remains partially engaged. Energy is consumed maintaining readiness rather than being released through resolution.

Emotional Exhaustion Without Obvious Cause

The pressure to remain responsive compounds this effect. When silence feels like neglect and disengagement feels risky, people stay partially attentive even during rest. Downtime becomes fragmented. Attention never fully stands down. The body and mind remain alert, waiting for the next cue.

Identity reinforcement also plays a role. When expression is tied to who one is perceived to be, maintaining consistency requires effort. People monitor themselves to ensure alignment with established cues. This monitoring is subtle, but it consumes energy over time. Authenticity begins to feel like maintenance rather than ease.

Because this work is externally prompted, people often misattribute the fatigue. They assume something is wrong with them. They search for personal explanations, such as poor time management, low resilience, or lack of discipline. The environmental contribution remains obscured because the demands are normalized.

Emotional exhaustion without obvious cause also reflects a loss of internal pacing. When systems regulate rhythm, people lose opportunities to calibrate their own limits. They respond when prompted rather than when ready. Over time, they become less able to sense when they need rest, disengagement, or quiet because those signals are overridden by external cues.

This exhaustion is not a sign of emotional weakness. It is a predictable response to sustained exposure without closure. Caring repeatedly without resolving. Reacting repeatedly without integrating. Remaining attentive without completing cycles. These conditions drain energy even in the absence of crisis.

The result is a dull fatigue rather than acute distress. People feel worn down rather than overwhelmed. They may still function well, but with less flexibility and less tolerance for ambiguity. Small demands feel heavier. Emotional range narrows. Recovery takes longer.

Recognizing this pattern matters because it reframes the problem. The issue is not that people care too much or think too little. It is that their emotional systems are being kept in a state of partial activation for extended periods without the structures needed for resolution.

The next chapter examines one of the mechanisms that makes this exhaustion harder to reverse. When reliance on external systems replaces internal pacing, people lose the ability to regulate their own emotional tempo. What once felt natural begins to feel inaccessible, even when the desire for balance remains.

LOSS OF INTERNAL PACING

CHAPTER 14
Loss of Internal Pacing

LOSS OF INTERNAL PACING

Loss of Internal Pacing

Internal pacing is the ability to regulate attention, emotion, and engagement according to one's own capacity. It allows people to speed up when necessary, slow down when overwhelmed, and pause without losing orientation. This pacing develops through repeated experience of starting, sustaining, and ending emotional and cognitive cycles. It is not a trait so much as a practiced skill.

In earlier environments, internal pacing was exercised constantly. People decided when to focus, when to disengage, and when to return. Emotional responses rose and fell in relation to events and were shaped by time, reflection, and social interaction. The rhythm of inner life was not perfectly controlled, but it was largely self-regulated.

Reliance on external systems changes this dynamic. When systems determine when attention should be activated, how long it should remain engaged, and when it should shift, internal pacing is used less often. The system provides timing cues that replace self-monitoring. Over time, people become accustomed to responding to prompts rather than to internal signals.

This shift is subtle. People do not consciously surrender pacing. They adapt. External cues feel helpful because they reduce uncertainty. They answer the question of what to attend to next and how intensely to care. In high-volume environments, this guidance feels efficient and stabilizing.

The cost of this efficiency appears gradually. Skills that are not practiced weaken. When internal pacing is rarely exercised, people become less sensitive to their own thresholds. They notice fatigue later. They push past limits without realizing it. Rest arrives only when exhaustion forces it.

Loss of internal pacing also affects emotional regulation. When systems dictate rhythm, emotions are experienced at externally set tempos. Peaks arrive quickly. Recovery is interrupted. Over time, people lose confidence in their ability to modulate feeling on their own. Calm feels passive rather than chosen. Intensity feels imposed rather than situational.

Loss Of Internal Pacing

This creates dependence. People begin to rely on external signals to tell them when it is acceptable to disengage or safe to re-engage. Silence feels unsettling. Absence of cues feels like disorientation rather than relief. Internal quiet loses its grounding function.

Without internal pacing, emotional self-trust erodes. People become uncertain about whether they are overreacting or underreacting. They look outward to calibrate response. This reinforces the system's role as regulator and further weakens internal capacity.

The loss of pacing also contributes to volatility. When people cannot gradually adjust intensity, shifts become abrupt. Engagement swings between overinvolvement and withdrawal. Emotional regulation feels inconsistent, even though the underlying issue is lack of practice rather than lack of control.

This pattern is often misread as instability. In reality, it reflects adaptation to environments that do not allow smooth modulation. People are responding to external tempo, not failing to manage their own.

Rebuilding internal pacing requires space. It requires periods where attention is not directed, emotion is not prompted, and urgency is not imposed. Without those conditions, internal regulation cannot reassert itself.

The next chapter explores what happens when externally regulated inner life becomes fragile. When systems that pace attention and emotion change, overload, or fail, people experience disruption that goes beyond inconvenience. The consequences reveal how much regulation has already been outsourced.

# CHAPTER 15
The Fragility of System-Regulated Inner Life

THE FRAGILITY OF SYSTEM-REGULATED INNER LIFE

The Fragility of System-Regulated Inner Life

When inner life is paced internally, disruption is uncomfortable but manageable. A stressful event passes. A routine is interrupted. Attention wobbles and then settles. People draw on practiced capacities to recalibrate. They may feel unsettled for a time, but they retain a sense of how to return to balance.

System-regulated inner life behaves differently. When systems carry a large share of the work of pacing attention and emotion, stability becomes contingent. Regulation depends on continuity of signals, familiar rhythms, and predictable feedback. When those conditions change, the effects are not limited to inconvenience or confusion. They register psychologically.

System changes are often abrupt. An update alters timing. A feed reorganizes priorities. Visibility patterns shift. Emotional cues that were once consistent disappear or invert. People notice changes in mood, focus, or reactivity without being able to explain why. The experience feels disproportionate to the technical adjustment because what has been disrupted is not content, but rhythm.

Overload produces similar effects. When too many signals arrive at once, the system's ability to pace emotion breaks down. Instead of guiding attention, it floods it. Urgency stacks without release. Emotional cues compete rather than sequence. People feel overwhelmed not because of any single demand, but because the regulating structure has failed to contain them.

In these moments, the absence of internal pacing becomes visible. Without external cues working smoothly, people struggle to regulate on their own. Attention feels scattered. Emotional intensity lingers without direction. The capacity to decide what matters falters because it has not been practiced under load.

This fragility often surprises people. They assume they should be able to adapt easily. When they cannot, they interpret the difficulty as personal weakness. In reality, they are experiencing withdrawal from a regulatory environment that had been doing more work than they realized.

The Fragility Of System-Regulated Inner Life

System failure can also take subtler forms. Delays, glitches, or inconsistency disrupt emotional expectation. Signals arrive out of order or not at all. The familiar cycle of activation and release is interrupted. People feel uneasy, restless, or irritable without a clear source. Inner life loses its cadence.

Because regulation was external, recovery is difficult. People wait for the system to stabilize rather than recalibrating themselves. Calm does not return automatically. Emotional equilibrium feels dependent on the restoration of familiar cues.

This dependency increases vulnerability. When regulation resides outside the individual, resilience depends on system reliability. Changes that would once have been absorbed now produce outsized effects. The inner life becomes sensitive to shifts it cannot control.

Fragility also appears when people attempt to disengage. Stepping away from system-paced environments can initially intensify distress. Without external rhythm, attention feels unanchored. Emotional quiet feels unfamiliar. People mistake this discomfort for evidence that disengagement is harmful, rather than recognizing it as the consequence of lost internal pacing.

This reaction discourages recovery. People return to the system not because it restores balance, but because it restores familiarity. The cycle reinforces itself. External regulation feels necessary because internal regulation has atrophied.

None of this implies that systems are inherently harmful or that dependence is a moral failing. It reflects a structural reality. When regulation is outsourced, capacity weakens. When capacity weakens, reliance deepens. Fragility emerges not from intention, but from design interacting with adaptation.

Recognizing this fragility is not a call to abandon systems. It is a call to understand where stability now resides. When inner life depends heavily on external pacing, disruption reveals how little margin remains.

The final chapter turns toward recovery. Reclaiming cognitive and emotional agency does not mean rejecting technology or withdrawing from shared spaces. It means restoring internal regulation so that systems no longer carry the full burden of pacing attention, emotion, and judgment.

CHAPTER 16
Reclaiming Cognitive and Emotional Agency

Reclaiming Cognitive and Emotional Agency

Reclaiming agency does not mean returning to an earlier era or rejecting the systems that now structure daily life. Systems are not optional, and they are not going away. The work is not withdrawal. It is rebalancing. Agency is reclaimed when internal capacities resume functions that have been quietly delegated, so that systems assist rather than determine the pacing of inner life.

The first step is recognition at a concrete level. Systems are not abstract forces. They are specific arrangements that decide timing, sequence, and emphasis. Feeds reorder themselves based on engagement velocity rather than completion or understanding. Notifications interrupt activity based on predicted responsiveness rather than necessity. Recommendation loops decide what comes next without asking whether anything has finished. Trending signals imply importance through visibility rather than consequence. Metrics reward reaction and ignore pause.

Each of these mechanisms performs work that people once did internally. They decide when attention should shift. They determine which emotions should be activated and how long they should last. They replace personal judgment about relevance with default continuation. None of this requires persuasion. The structure itself carries authority.

Recognizing this changes the problem. People stop treating exhaustion, reactivity, or distraction as personal failings and begin to see them as predictable responses to environments that continuously manage sequence and tempo. Agency is not lost because people stopped caring or thinking. It is diluted because the order of operations was changed.

Insourcing begins by restoring that order. Insourcing attention does not mean paying more attention or consuming less information. It means reclaiming when attention starts and stops. Instead of being summoned by refresh, alert, or interruption, attention is entered deliberately. A feed is something one goes to, not something that arrives. A thought is allowed to finish before a new stimulus is accepted. Attention is permitted to idle without immediate replacement, even when idling feels unfamiliar or slightly uncomfortable.

This idling is not empty. It is where integration occurs. When attention is not immediately redirected, impressions settle. Emotional tone becomes clearer. Importance begins to decay naturally rather than being artificially sustained. What remains often matters more than what disappears.

Insourcing emotional pacing follows a similar reversal. Instead of converting feeling directly into expression or reaction, emotion is allowed to run its course internally. Anger is noticed without being immediately discharged. Concern is tolerated without being escalated. Anxiety is held long enough to reveal whether it is situational or residual.

This feels difficult at first because systems have trained rapid offloading. Expression has become the endpoint of feeling. When that outlet is delayed, emotion can intensify briefly. That intensity is often mistaken for evidence that expression is necessary. In reality, it is the sensation of a cycle that has not been allowed to complete on its own.

When emotions are allowed to resolve internally, they often change shape. Urgency softens. Outrage becomes specificity. Fear becomes information. This does not happen because emotions are suppressed, but because they are finished rather than interrupted.

Insourcing judgment requires reclaiming the right not to evaluate everything that appears. Systems flatten importance by presenting all stimuli in the same temporal frame. Insourcing restores hierarchy. Some things are allowed to matter less without justification. Some issues are acknowledged without response. Some concerns are permitted to fade without being replaced.

This is not apathy. It is proportion. Judgment regains strength when absence is allowed to mean resolution or irrelevance rather than neglect. When people decide explicitly what does not require response, mental load decreases. The constant sense of pending obligation begins to lift because obligation is once again chosen rather than assumed.

Insourcing moral attention builds on this. Awareness is separated from responsibility. Knowing about something no longer implies that one must react, condemn, or align publicly. Care is reconnected to capacity. Moral concern becomes sustainable when it is bounded.

This boundary-setting often triggers discomfort at first. Systems have trained moral responsiveness to feel continuous. Stepping back can feel like moral failure. Over time, however, people rediscover that restraint preserves care. Moral energy becomes deeper and more durable when it is not constantly drained by reaction without agency.

Identity also shifts when insourcing takes hold. When expression is no longer continuously reinforced by visibility and feedback, people regain room to experience themselves privately. Mixed feelings are allowed to coexist without resolution. Positions can change internally before they are declared, or without being declared at all.

This loosening restores flexibility. Identity becomes something that develops rather than something that must be maintained through consistent signaling. People feel less pressure to react in ways that confirm who they have been and more freedom to notice what they are actually thinking or feeling now.

None of this requires abandoning systems or adopting rigid rules. It requires reassigning roles. Systems continue to provide information, connection, and access. What changes is that they no longer decide sequence by default. Attention is not constantly preempted. Emotion is not constantly cued. Judgment is not constantly prompted.

Agency returns gradually, through use. Internal pacing strengthens as it is practiced. Emotional cycles become more complete. Exhaustion eases not because demands disappear, but because engagement regains structure. People recover the ability to speed up when circumstances require it and slow down when they do not.

This work does not produce permanent calm or perfect balance. Cognitive and emotional agency are not stable traits. They are capacities that strengthen with use and weaken with neglect. In environments designed for outsourcing, reclaiming them is an ongoing practice rather than a one-time correction.

Understanding this reframes the broader experience described throughout this book. Exhaustion, reactivity, urgency, and fragility are not signs of personal failure. They are predictable outcomes of environments that quietly absorbed work once done internally. Recovery does not require fixing oneself. It requires restoring functions that were never meant to be fully externalized.

Outsourced thinking did not happen all at once, and it cannot be reversed all at once. But awareness changes posture. Reassignment restores sequence. Over time, people rediscover that they can pace their own attention, regulate their own emotional tempo, and decide what deserves judgment without constant guidance.

That is what agency looks like now. Not independence from systems, but the ability to remain oriented within them without surrendering the structure of inner life.

THE END

www.ingramcontent.com/pod-product-compliance
Lightning Source LLC
Chambersburg PA
CBHW070642030426
42337CB00020B/4125